BOSCO
And the Rainbow Bridge

Written by Debra Couwenberg
With illustrations by Susan Duncan

Based on a story by Rita Ann Freeman

A note to our readers

Bosco's journey over the Rainbow Bridge is a heartfelt tale of love, friendship, and the unbreakable bond between pets and their families. At WhiskerTorium™, we cherish these special connections and understand how challenging it can be to say goodbye to a beloved friend.

Our mission is to support families and help children navigate the feelings that come with losing a pet. We believe that through stories like Bosco's, we can open our hearts and start conversations that heal.

To explore more stories, resources and ways to celebrate the pets we hold dear, we invite you to visit us at whiskertorium.com

With warmth and understanding

The WhiskerTorium™ Family

Just outside the gates of Heaven,
Is a place called "The Rainbow Bridge",
Rolling hills of sweet, green grass are
Sprinkled with lush shade trees, brooks and ponds.

When their life on Earth is through,
Our pets just 'wake up' there one day,
Even if they are old, ill or infirm,
Each is restored to youthful vigor and wholeness.

They have all the food and treats they need,
Fresh, cool water to drink,
As they play happily with each other,
Among the meadows of The Rainbow Bridge.

Until one special day comes for each of them....

Bosco loved dreaming.
Sometimes he dreamed of playing with other dogs or chasing squirrels. Sometimes, he dreamed of running with his human who he called Mummy.

His little feet would move in his sleep, and once in a while, he even barked. Sometimes, he would kick Mummy in his sleep, waking her up. She didn't always like that part.

Every day, Bosco spent time with Mummy. He watched her from room to room, guarding the house, and especially watching for sneaky squirrels. His favourite thing was when Mummy would sit in the big chair with him, telling him what a good boy he was while stroking his back.

Bosco had spent many happy years with Mummy. But now he was getting older, and his hip hurt. He couldn't jump or run like he used to, but every day still felt special.

One day, Bosco woke up from a nap, but something was different. Instead of Mummy's house, he found himself in a huge, grassy field.

The soft grass felt cool under his paws, and far off, he saw birds flying in circles. Bosco's legs felt strong and fast again! He raced toward the birds, filled with excitement.

As Bosco ran, he saw a big oak tree with birds chirping in its branches. Nearby, there was a sparkling pond. He trotted over and took a big, cool drink of water. Then, he noticed something wonderful—there was a pile of his favorite treats next to the pond! While Bosco was enjoying his treats, he heard a voice. "You're new here, aren't you?"

Bosco looked around but saw no one. "Up here!" the voice said. Bosco looked up at the oak tree and saw the tree smiling down at him! "I'm Birdie Tree," the tree said. "Welcome to the Rainbow Bridge."

Bosco was confused. "What's the Rainbow Bridge?" he asked. "It's a special place for animals like you. You get to wait here until your person comes," Birdie explained kindly.

As Bosco looked around, he noticed more animals gathering near the pond–dogs, cats, even a horse and a llama! A sleek white cat approached Bosco. "Welcome to the Rainbow Bridge! You'll like it here," the cat said. "I'm Romeo, by the way." A golden retriever with a soft Southern voice added, "We're all waiting for our people to come so we can cross the bridge together."

"Where does the bridge go?" Bosco asked. "It crosses the river that leads to Heaven," Birdie said. "And when your person comes, you'll cross together." Bosco's heart ached a little. "But I miss Mummy already! I want to see her!". Romeo smiled. "You can still check on her. Just look into the gazing pond."

Bosco did as Romeo said. He peered into the water, and to his surprise, he saw Mummy! She looked so sad. Bosco's heart sank. "She doesn't know where I am," he whispered. Birdie spoke softly. "You can visit her in her dreams, Bosco. It's a special gift. You can show her the Rainbow Bridge and let her know you're okay." Bosco's eyes lit up. "I want to do that!"

That night, Bosco appeared in Mummy's dream. He showed her the beautiful meadow, the trees and the Rainbow Bridge over the sparkling river. He told her, "It's real, Mummy! The Rainbow Bridge is real! I'm here, and I'll be waiting for you." In her dream, Mummy smiled through her tears. Bosco gently kicked his feet, hoping she would feel it in real life.

When Bosco woke up by the gazing pond, he rushed to look into the water again. This time, when he saw Mummy, she wasn't crying anymore. She was telling her grandchildren about the dream she had. "Bosco is waiting for me at the Rainbow Bridge," she said. "One day, we'll be together again."

Bosco's tail wagged with joy. He knew Mummy would be okay, and one day, when she walked that special path, he would greet her with all the love in his heart.

She understood the Rainbow Bridge now—where Bosco would be patiently waiting for her. And when that day came, they would be together again... forever and always.

 Debra Couwenberg is a compassionate storyteller and devoted animal lover from Western Canada. A single mother to her daughter Dini, Debra faced the hardships of loss early in life, losing both of her parents by the time Dini was just two months old. Throughout these difficult times, her animals were her solace. Having shared her life with many pets Debra understands the profound healing power they offer.

She views their passing as the loss of a beloved family member, knowing firsthand the pain that comes with it. A lifelong pet parent, Debra has shared her home with a wide variety of animals, including two chicks (with a funny story to match), guinea pigs, rats (mommas and babies from her biology class over Christmas), cats, dogs, fish and birds. Currently she lives with two beloved cats, Peaches and Luke. The loss of her cherished Devon Rex, Diva, deeply impacted her as Diva passed away in Debra's arms. This experience with grief led Debra to discover Bosco and the Rainbow Bridge, a short story by Rita Ann Freeman. Deeply moved by its message, Debra saw the potential to adapt it into a children's book to help families with young children cope with the loss of a pet in a gentle and meaningful way. With permission and copyright, she transformed the story into a beautifully illustrated children's book, ensuring its comforting message could reach fur baby families everywhere. Through Bosco and the Rainbow Bridge, Debra hopes to provide comfort and healing to children and families, helping them cherish the love and memories of their pets that never fade.

Debra believes that every pet leaves a lasting paw print on our hearts, and she is committed to helping others through the difficult journey of losing a furry companion. In addition to her work as an author, she founded WhiskerTorium™, a company that honours pets who have passed by offering discreet, beautifully crafted urns and keepsakes. A portion of the proceeds from both WhiskerTorium™ and Bosco and the Rainbow Bridge is donated to support animals in need.

To learn more about Debra and her work, visit WhiskerTorium.ca, @WhiskerTorium, BoscoAndTheRainbowBridge.com, @BoscoAndTheRainbowBridge

Copyright © 2024 , WhiskerTorium™

All rights reserved. No part of this publication may be reproduced, stored in a retrieval system or transmitted in any form or by any means electronic, mechanical, photocopying, recording or otherwise, without the express and prior written consent of the author or publisher.